IN THIS GUIDE WE DESCRIBE THE HABITS OF EACH BUG, PRESCRIBING PROBLEM INSECT CONTROL METHODS & RECIPES THAT YOU CAN MAKE YOURSELF.

People have said these DIY remedies work. For instance, we know that beer and masking tape works in controlling cockroaches and we are pretty sure this method has not been tested in any university, but it does work.

This book is written in a scientific format using scientific entomological names, (hopefully not to annoy you). It's so anyone can check them out for more information if they want.

We've made it easy for everyone to understand. Discussing each pest in detail and letting you know how they're different and how they need different methods of control. In some cases we lumped several closely related pests together.

THE CONCERNED CITIZENS

CITIZENS

SAFE PEST CONTROL GUIDE

COMMON HOUSEHOLD PESTS

BRISTLETAILS (THYSANURA)

Silverfish and firebrats are the only two insects from this order that become pests and firebrats are not common in homes. **True bristletails (Machilidae)** are almost always found outside.

Silverfish (Lepismatidae – Lepisma saccharina)

Silverfish are small insects, up to ¾ inch long and silvery in color. They are covered in scales, which will be hard to see with the naked eye, and they have three appendages protruding from their abdomen.

They feed on fungus, sugar and starch products such as flour, glue and paste. They can feed on some synthetic fabrics and cellulose which includes paper, books, photographs and cardboard boxes. They will also feed on dead insects.

Silverfish are attracted to moisture so you want to make sure you fix any plumbing leaks as soon as possible. They are frequently found in crawl spaces under a home if it is damp there. You have to make sure no moisture is available for these insects and try to keep items such as paper, books, and food products as far from the floor as possible.

DIY Tip: How you can trap Silverfish.

- Put some flour in a glass jar.
- Wrap with duct tape, so they can climb up the sides. They will get in the jar, but will not be able to get out.

For more information about Anura Organic Insect Control and our full line of products please visit our website at: **OrganicPestStore.com**

Cockroaches often enter homes by hitching rides inside food products, boxes, paper bags and any used furniture or appliances. It's best to inspect these items for egg capsules before you bring them inside. In addition you should seal any holes or crevices around plumbing under sinks and behind toilets. Regularly vacuum and clean floors under the kitchen appliances.

Keep all of your drains closed at night to prevent them from coming up from the sewer system. Also, get your attic and crawlspace, (if you have them,) dusted with food-grade diatomaceous earth.

American cockroaches (Blattidae - Periplaneta americana)

This roach feeds on a wide variety of plant and animal material and it's commonly found in sewer systems, coming up the drains at night and enter the living space of homes. It also likes crawl spaces under the home. In some parts of the country, particularly the southeast, they frequently live outside, reaching a little over 1 ½ inches in length. They are dark brown with a yellowish band around its thorax (section behind head).

DIY Tip: Two methods that work best to control roaches:

- *Put equal amounts of baking soda and sugar out in a flat lid and they will gobble it up.*

How to make roach bait dough balls:

1. *Combine ½ c. powdered sugar and ¼ c. shortening or bacon drippings.*
2. *Add ½ c. onions, ½ c. flour and 8 oz. baking soda.*
3. *Add enough water to make a dough-like consistency.*
4. *Make balls out of the bait and put them wherever you see roaches.*

Australian cockroaches (Blattidae - Periplaneta australasiae)

The Australian cockroach is similar to the American cockroach, but is slightly smaller. The yellow markings on the thorax are much more distinct on this roach and it has a yellowish marking on the outer edge of each wing or the "shoulder. It is found from central Florida to east. Texas in the south. It has been found in some northern states, but usually in greenhouse environments. They normally infest the attics and crawl spaces of homes and then wander in the living areas for food.

Control tip:

- *Dust your attic and crawl spaces with food-grade diatomaceous earth.*
- *Niban Bait works well with these roaches.*

Oriental cockroaches (Blattidae - Blatta orientalis)

Oriental cockroaches or "waterbugs" are found throughout the United States but they aren't seen very often in the southeastern states. They are about an inch long. The female is all black and the male has two brown wing tips, but it cannot fly. These roaches are common in sewer systems and will come up the drains into the homes. They are also common under ground debris outside and love stacks of firewood. These roaches will readily take Niban Bait as well as the homemade baits discussed above.

Turkestan cockroaches (Blattidae - Blatta lateralis)

Turkestan cockroaches are closely related to Oriental roaches. They are about in inch in length with color variations between the male and female. Males are red/brown with pale or white lateral stripes on the ventral side of the wing base. The male also has wings that cover the entire abdomen. Females are dark brown in color with short lateral white dashes at end of the wing. The female wings are very short in comparison to the male and do not cover the entire abdomen.

Brown-banded cockroaches (Blatellidae - Supella longipalpa)

Brown-banded cockroaches are about a half inch long. Males are light brown while the female has dark brown wings. Both sexes have light colored bands running across the wings. These roaches do not require as much water as German roaches and will often be found in bedrooms and living rooms. The roach baits described above will work on these insects.

German cockroaches (Blatellidae - Blatella germanica)

The German cockroach is the most prolific of the roaches. It is small, dark brown with two distinct black stripes on its thorax. It will feed on almost anything edible and a lot of things we wouldn't consider edible. They go from egg to adult in as little as 45 days and, if left unchecked, can severely infest a home or business. Usually they are most commonly found in kitchens and bathrooms.

German cockroaches are also believed capable of transmitting staphylococcus, streptococcus and coliform bacteria and are known to be responsible for many allergy and asthma problems. In addition, German cockroaches have been implicated in the increase of asthma and the spread of typhoid, dysentery and leprosy organisms. Living roaches, dead roaches, roach feces, saliva, cast skins, cockroach eggs and their decaying body parts all contain allergens which can contaminate the air with aeroallergens and cause allergic reactions in people.

Control tip: German cockroaches will eat almost anything, but keeping the house clean and free of moisture will help:

- *Seal any small openings with caulk, and make sure your home is moisture free, as much as possible.*

- *Mix vinegar and water together into a household sprayer and spray to deter any roaches.*

- *Lemon Juice mixed with water is another scent that drives roaches away.*

- *To control German roaches, you should use German Roach Pheromone Traps as well as some of the baits. The traps will attract and catch the roaches.*

ANTS (HYMENOPTERA – FORMICIDAE)

There are about 570 species of ants in the United States. Of those, about 30 species are common household pests. When discussing ants, we will use three terms that reflect the size of the ants in a colony.

1. **Monomorphic,** this means all the workers are the same size.

2. **Bimorphic,** means they have two sizes in the colony. The larger ones are major workers and the smaller ones are minor workers.

3. **Polymorphic,** means they have three or more sizes of workers in the colony.

Basic Ant Control Steps: There are several things you can do to prevent ants from entering your home. The first step is exclusion.

1. Go around the outside of your home and inspect it very carefully from an ant's point of view. Ants can sense cool air and aromatic odors emanating from your home and will try to gain access.

2. Check around the house at ground level and look for cracks in the foundation, voids around pipes, areas under stucco, peepholes in bricks and similar areas that ants can use to gain entrance.

3. Caulk all these areas, or otherwise alter the perimeter to prevent ants from using it to get into your home.

4. Check around your windows and doors to make sure they close tightly. If the doors aren't tight, you may have to install door sweeps on them.

5. Check your bushes, shrubs and trees to make sure you don't have any branches touching the roof.

6. Don't stack firewood, bricks or anything else next to your house or ants and other insects may find a good place to nest.

7. If you have bushes or shrubs next to your house, periodically inspect them for aphids, scales and similar bugs. Ants are attracted to the honeydew they produce.

8. Don't put flagstone or flat boards on the ground too close to your home or some species of ants will nest under them.

DIY Tip: Here is a list of repellents that have been shown to be effective:
Cinnamon • Baking soda • Comet Cleanser • Medicated baby powder • Tide • Talcum powder • Chalk • Coffee grounds • Borax • Garlic • Broken egg shells • Bone meal • Black or red pepper • Peppermint • Paprika • Chili powder • Mint leaves.

There are three groups (Subfamilies) of ants that have pest (or guest) species. They are **Myrmicinae, Dolichodorinae** and **Formicinae.**

DIY bait trap tips: Simple recipe for effective, homemade ant baits/traps. First you will need:

1. *3 cups of water, 1 cup of sugar, 1 tsp. borax or 2 tsp. food-grade DE, 6 small screw-top jelly jars with lids.*
2. *Cover the jars with masking tape, this will enable the ants to climb up.*
3. *Mix sugar, water and borax in a bowl.*
4. *Loosely half-fill the jars with cotton balls or pieces of sponge or wadded paper towels.*
5. *Pour up to ½ cup of the sugary mixture over the cotton balls, saturating them.*
6. *Make several small holes in the lid. Screw the lids on the jars tightly.*

- *You can also use instant grits, which they can't digest or use 2 packets of Equal or NutraSweet, which contains aspartame, on ant trails.*

DIY Tips for ants invading your pantry: If the ants are eating your apple sauce, peanut butter, canned cat food, Karo Syrup, jelly or similar products:

- *Mix in small amounts of boric acid or borax or aspartame.*
- *Mix about 2% of any of these products in the food.*
- <u>Make sure you keep these baits away from children and pets.</u>
- *If the ants are dying near the baits, you are making it too strong and need to make a fresh batch with less boric acid or borax.*

DIY Tips for ants making mounds in your yard:
- *Flood the nests with club soda or with white vinegar or food-grade diatomaceous earth. If you use the diatomaceous earth, mix 4 tablespoons per gallon of water.*
- *You can also use 1 gallon of orange juice diluted with 2 gallons of water and a dash of soap.*
- *If you prefer, you can also spread dry instant grits on the mound. The ants will eat it and not be able to digest it and die.*

Please Note: If you smoke, always wear plastic gloves when making ant baits or they will sense the tobacco smoke on the baits and not go to it. Ants do not like cigarette or cigar smoke.

Repellent spray tip: If you are finding ants in a classroom or office building and baits aren't practical, then you can spray the ouside foundation with Anura Organic Insect Control, which is a cedar oil product and it will kill the ants it hits while repelling any others.

Big-headed ants (Myrmicinae - Pheidole spp.)

Big-headed ants are bimorphic seed gatherers. The minor workers look like average ants. They gather the seeds and the major workers, with the enlarged heads, break them open. The major workers also defend the colony. These ants usually have small colonies of a couple of hundred ants. Occasionally they'll come in a house, but they won't hurt anything.

Acrobat ants (Myrmicinae - Crematogaster spp.)

Acrobat ants don't do anything acrobatic, except occasionally running around on four legs instead of all six. Acrobat ants are small, usually red and black, but there are all black species as well. The abdomen (last segment) appears flat on top when viewed from the side and is spade-shaped when viewed from above. There are two small spines on the thorax (segment between the head and abdomen). Acrobat ants are found over most of the United States.

Acrobats normally feed on the honeydew secretion of aphids that infest plants near your home. They may enter your home from the roof when branches touch the house. They will get between latillas and kick out a lot of loose sawdust. It looks like they are doing damage, but they aren't. They are simply making a mess.

DIY Tip: They will readily take sweet baits.

- To make a bait, use honey or Karo Syrup mixed with 2% boric acid or borax.

- Terro Ant Bait is also a very good commercial ant bait.

Little black ants (Myrmicinae - Monomorium minimum)

This species is commonly called "little black ants, which is confusing as there are several species of little (small) black ants. Monomorium minimum are very small, shiny black ants that are monomorphic. These ants are found throughout the United States and southern Canada. Usually they nest outdoors where they can feed on the honeydew secretion of some insects, but occasionally they infest homes. In a home they will eat whatever is available, including bread, meats, sweets, fruits and vegetables. They will bite to protect themselves.

DIY Tip: How to make the Little Black Ant peanut butter & jelly bait:

- Take two tablespoons each of peanut butter and jelly mixed with one tablespoon of boric acid or borax.

Pharaoh ants (Myrmicinae - Monomorium pharaonis)

These very small, yellowish ants are monomorphic. Originally discovered and described in Egypt in 1758, (hence their name.) They are now found in many areas of the United States, nesting in any small, dark voids such as old boxes, empty bags, stacked newspapers, wall voids, under flooring, and/or especially near hot water pipes or heating systems. Outdoors they will nest under objects on the ground, in potted plants, in stacked firewood or piles of bricks. Pharaoh ants are primarily nocturnal, coming out to feed at night.

Colonies, often exceed a quarter of a million ants and a couple of hundred queens. Unlike most other ant species they do not swarm to reproduce, but using a system called "budding." This is where reproductives just crawl off and mate nearby. It's important to note: Colonies usually contain many nests and it is essential to control all of them or you will never get rid of them.

Never use synthetic pesticides in trying to control these ants as all you will do is cause them to split up, making the problem worse.

Pharaoh ants are a major pest in hospitals where they have been associated with over 20 disease-causing pathogenic organisms.

They will enter isolation wards, operating rooms and patient rooms where they feed on blood and blood products and then contaminate sterile areas.

They are not native to the western U.S. and are brought in on commerce. They normally infest apartment complexes, hospitals and large commercial buildings in this area.

They rarely infest homes, but it isn't impossible.

DIY Tips: How to make the Pharaoh Ant straw baits:

1. Mix half fruit juice with half aspartame and place inside soda straws.

2. Cut the straws into one inch segments and put the segments where you have seen the pharaoh ants foraging.

3. You can even tape them to the underside of tables.

- For better effect, change the baits periodically by mixing peanut oil, sweet syrup, jelly or honey with 3% boric acid or food grade diatomaceous earth.

Note: Place the straw filled baits as close to the nests as possible.

- You can also put strained liver baby food, honey or peanut butter mixed with 2% boric acid or borax in beer caps.

- For best results, treat any cracks and crevices around the outside of the home with Anura Organic Insect Control.

Harvester ants (Myrmicinae - Pogonomyrmex spp.)

This group of ants are commonly called "Harvester ants. They are comparatively large, 3/16" - 1/2" long, red to dark brown in color and they have a pair of spines on their thorax. They have a stinger and will use it if disturbed. Harvester ants are bimorphic. They make large mounds covered in gravel which retains heat and helps incubate the eggs in the nest below. These ants feed on seeds, which they gather for the winter. While harvester ants are considered aggressive, in reality they are only defensive.

During mating season, usually in late July or early August, swarmers from a harvester ant colony will fly high in the air.

Control Tip: The best product to use to control harvester ants is Niban Bait, a commercial grain-like bait that's made from boric acid.

Fire ants (Myrmicinae - Solenopsis invicta)

The imported fire ants can be very dangerous. They are polymorphic and reddish-brown to black in color. They have severe stings that can cause blisters and allergic responses to the venom as well as anaphylactic shock.

Over 30,000 people a year in this country seek medical attention from the stings of these ants.

Fire ants have been found in Florida, Georgia, South Carolina, North Carolina, Tennessee, Alabama, Arizona, New Mexico, Mississippi, California, Louisiana, Arkansas, Texas and Oklahoma.

Fire ant mounds can be 2 feet in diameter and a foot and a half high, with a single colony containing close to a quarter of a million ants.

Fire ants will eat both plant and animal products, including rodents and some reptiles. They will feed on a wide variety of plants, including strawberries, potatoes and corn. Queens in the colony need proteins, so when you mix baits make sure they're protein-based. These ants are attracted to magnetic fields and will get in transformers, air conditioners and other electrical equipment. One good thing about fire ants is that they like to feed on ticks, fleas, cockroaches and flies.

DIY Tips: To keep fire ants out of electrical equipment outside:

- Dust with food-grade diatomaceous earth, this will keep the ants out of these areas.
- For a bait, you can mix a tablespoon of boric acid or aspartame with 2 tablespoons of sugar, jelly, honey or pet food.
- You can flood their nests with one gallon of orange juice mixed with two gallons of water and a cup of dish soap.

Thief ants (Myrmicinae - Solenopsis molesta)

Thief ants are very small ants that are related to fire ants, but resemble pharaoh ants. They are less than 1/16th of an inch long. The best way to tell them from pharaoh ants is to examine the antennae with a magnifying glass. The club on the end of the antennae has two segments in thief ants and three segments in pharaoh ants. Thief ants get their name from their habit of entering the colonies of other ant species and stealing their food.

These ants are found throughout the United States but are more common in the east and south. Outside, they nest under debris on the ground, or under rocks, boards or logs. In a home, they will nest in wall voids and behind baseboards.

DIY Tips: Baits do not work well for these ants as they don't bring enough back to the colony for it to work.
- *For best results you need to find the ant nest, and put some food-grade diatomaceous earth in the void.*
- *Sprinkle cinnamon to repel thief ants in areas you don't want them.*
- *You can also spray all the cracks and crevices around the outside of your home with Anura Organic Insect Control to keep them out.*

Pavement ants (Myrmicinae -Tetramorium caespitum)

Pavement ants are small, monomorphic, brown to black ants covered in small stiff hairs. The head and thorax are covered with small grooves that are easy to see. There are two small spines on the thorax.

These ants frequently nest under concrete foundation slabs, entering the home through the expansion joints, or where plumbing penetrates the slab. Once inside, they will nest inside walls or other voids, often close to a heating source for warmth.

They originated in Europe and are now found throughout much of the U. S. and are major pests in the northeast and midwest. They are also common in areas of California and New Mexico. They can sting and bite if disturbed. Pavement ants feed on the honeydew secretion of aphids and other insects as well as on seeds. They have very large colonies.

DIY Tips: Pavement ants readily take baits.
- *Mix two tablespoons of peanut butter and jelly or honey with a tablespoon of boric acid or borax. Then place on active ant trails.*
- *If you can find their nest, dust it with food-grade diatomaceous earth.*
- *Or spray it to the dripping point with Anura Organic Insect Control.*

Argentine ants (Dolichoderinae - Linepithema humile)

Argentine ants are small, monomorphic and brown in color. They are one of the most successful ants species on the planet. They have huge colonies and when they move into urban areas, they displace native ant species.

Unlike other ants who fight when they encounter other colonies of their same species, Argentine ants will merge and form super-colonies, and in some cases, mega-colonies.

There is one mega-colony of Argentine ants in Europe that extends over 3,700 miles and encompasses parts of Spain, Portugal, France and Italy.

This mega-colony is estimated to contain hundreds of billions of ants. They were first found in California in 1905 near Ontario, it's now found in almost all urban areas of California where it's a major household pest. Besides California and Louisiana, there are records of these ants in Utah, New Mexico, South Dakota, Arkansas, Illinois, Florida, Alabama and Hawaii.

DIY Tips for indoors: Argentine ant workers have a sweet tooth, so indoors use this sweet bait formula to place on the active ant trails:

- Mix honey or light Karo Syrup with aspartame or 2% boric acid or borax.
- To make peanut butter baits, just add 2% boric acid, or you could use borax. The Queens need high protein to function so this works well.

Keep all of these baits away from children and pets.

- You can also sprinkle the most active areas with baking soda, Comet, Tide laundry soap, talcum powder or food grade diatomaceous earth.
- If you see ant trails, spray them with bleach or vinegar.

Control Tips for outdoors: Never spray pesticides on the ants as all you will do is kill a few and the rest will go to other areas of the house. The best commercial product is Anura Organic Insect Control. This will repel most ants including Argentine ants.

1. Spray this around your foundation every couple of days for a while.
2. After a couple of weeks, spray it once a week. Soon you can do it every two or three weeks. It doesn't have the residual power of a pesticide, but it isn't dangerous either.
3. Also; Remove all mulch (other than aromatic cedar mulch) from around the foundation of the building. Seal all cracks and crevices. Do not let any branches touch the building.

- If you find the nest outdoors, a good DIY method is to flood it with orange juice mixed with soapy water.

Pyramid ants (Dolichoderinae - Dorymyrmex spp.)

Pyramid ants are reddish-brown or black and are monomorphic. They have a distinct pyramid-shaped projection on the back of their thorax, hence their name. These small ants rarely come into homes. They usually make many small mounds around the yard and in cracks in sidewalks and on patios.

They are found in most of the southern states and in California.

DIY Tips: How to make sweet ant baits.

- If the Pyramid ants come indoors, mix equal parts of jelly or honey with aspartame. **Note:** It's important to place the bait on the ant trails.
- For outdoors, pour a cup of baking soda on the mounds, wait about a half an hour and pour a cup of vinegar on the mounds.
- You can also pour a 2-litre bottle of Coca Cola or Club Soda down the mound. Push a stick into the mound entrance and move it around to make the hole larger before pouring the Coca Cola or Club Soda in.
- Terro bait is a good commercial bait.

Odorous house ants (Dolichoderinae -Tapinoma sessile)

Odorous house ants are small dark reddish-brown to black ants and are monomorphic. They will follow each other in single file when entering a building. Outside they nest under objects such as rocks, boards, or any
kind of debris. When they come in the home, they can nest in wall voids. If the house has a crawl space, they will nest in that area and come into the house to forage for food and water. Odorous house ants have multiple queens in a colony and hence, have large colonies.

They are probably the most common ant found in homes in the U.S., except in areas where Argentine ants live. They do not bite or sting. The body of the odorous house ant is relatively soft and can be easily crushed. When this occurs, a very unpleasant "coconut" odor is apparently released. I can say that in over 40 years I have never sniffed an ant so can't vouch for the smell. An average Odorous House Ant colony will have 10,000 to 40,000 members and several queens. Mating and swarming takes place in the nest and new colonies are formed by budding.

DIY Tips: How to make a good bait for controlling these ants.

- Mix two tablespoons each of peanut butter and jelly mixed with a tablespoon of boric acid or borax. Place on the ant trails.
- A good commercial bait is Terro Ant Bait which is made from boric acid.
- Treat areas where they are entering your home outside with Anura Organic Insect Control, which is a cedarwood oil product.

White-footed ants (Dolichoderinae -Technomyrmex difficilis)

White-footed ants are small, black ants with white hind legs. They are monomorphic. These ants are one of the hardest species to control. The primary reason is their wingless reproduction, reproducing faster than almost any other species of ants as they have so many queens laying eggs. Some colonies can contain up to 3 million ants and half of these can be reproductive. The good news is that they don't bite, sting or cause any damage. They're simply a nuisance by their numbers.

These ants are found in Florida, South Carolina, Louisiana, California and in Montreal, Quebec, Canada.

White-footed ants feed on the nectar of some plants and the honeydew secretion of aphids and similar insects. Outdoors, white-footed ants can be found under the bark of trees or even in the old galleries of termites in wooden structures. They can also live in compost piles, leaf litter, under rocks and in outdoor furniture. They can move into homes and nest in attics, under roof shingles, in walls, and similar areas. One colony can have several colonies in or around a single home.

Control tip: The best way to deal with White-footed Ants:

- Indoors, remove their food source of any water and sweet liquids. Caulk all cracks and crevices around the foundation.

- Caulk all small openings in windows and doors.

- Spray plants or shrubs that have aphids with Anura Organic Insect Control to help remove food source.

- Spray Anura Organic Insect Control around your foundation once a month to create a continuous barrier around the outside of your home.

- Drench white-footed ant mounds with the same concentrate.

Yellow ants (Formicinae - Acanthomyops spp)

Yellow ants are medium size ants and are yellow in color. They are monomorphic. These ants are found throughout the Midwest and New England and more commonly in the southern states including Texas and New Mexico. They feed on the honeydew secretion of aphids and similar insects. They will nest under debris on the ground around a house and in foundation walls but rarely forage in a home.

Control tip: Rarely a problem in a home, but if they are take these steps:
- If they come in the house, use a sweet bait mixture of honey or light Karo Syrup with aspartame or 2% boric acid or borax.

- Spray the foundation with Anura Organic Insect Control.

Carpenter ants (Formicinae - Camponotus spp)

Carpenter ants are large, polymorphic and are black, reddish-brown, red and black or light brown in color, depending on the species. The thorax is evenly convex when viewed from the side. That differentiates them from field ants who are also large but have an indented thorax. Field ants are rarely household pests.

Carpenter ants are found throughout the United States. There are a number of known species. Five species that are common include **Camponotus pennsylvanicus, Camponotus modoc, Camponotus herculeanus, Camponotus laevigatus** and **Camponotus vicinus.**

Most species are active in the late afternoons and at night. They will nest under the slabs of homes and enter through expansion joints or around plumbing. They are also found in crawl spaces under homes, generally found in areas where there's moisture. If there's damp wood available, they will make galleries, destroying structural wood to make their nests. They don't eat the wood, they just carve out areas and create wood segments (frass). If they are in the house, they will forage for any foods available, including pet foods, candies, syrups, sugar and other sweet products. They will also feed on any fruits they encounter and will root through the garbage looking for grease, fat or meat scraps.

DIY Tips: The most effective way of eliminating Carpenter Ants.
- *Mix two tablespoons each of honey or jelly mixed with a tablespoon of boric acid or borax. Then place on active ant trails.*

- Keep out of the reach of children and pets.

Crazy ants (Formicinae - Paratrechina longicornis)

Crazy ants are black or brown, appear thin and have very long legs, running around erratically, giving them their name. They are monomorphic.

These ants are found along the coasts of California and southern Oregon in the west. Originally from India, they do well in a variety of habitats, including areas that are very dry to areas that are wet. You'll find their nest under wood, in tree cavities, in or under any debris left on the ground for a long time and even in potted plants. This ant species reproduces by budding rather than by swarming.

Crazy ants feed on a variety of foods, including sweets and even other insects. They particularly like house flies when they can catch them. They will also feed on the honeydew secretion from aphids and scales.

DIY Tips:

- *Mix two tablespoons each of honey or jelly mixed with a tablespoon of boric acid or borax. Then place on active ant trails.*

- *They love garbage, so make sure garbage storage areas are as clean as possible.*

- *Put food grade diatomaceous earth around the house under any bushes or shrubs.*

- *If you can find the nest, spray it with a good natural pesticide such as Anura Organic Insect Control, this will help control them.*

WASPS &YELLOWJACKETS (HYMENOPTERA)

There are a number of species of wasps and yellowjackets that you may encounter, but the habits and control methods of most of them is the same. If you can't live with them in your yard, you probably should call a professional as they (wasps and yellowjackets) can be dangerous if disturbed or threatened.

Paper wasps (Vespidae; Polistinae - Polistes spp.)

A paper wasp queen is the lone reproductive female, who begins her nest by attaching a thick paper strand to an overhanging structure or protective site. She then builds hollow paper cells by chewing wood or plant fibers (cellulose) mixed with water. There are 27 species in North America that are considered semi-social.

The grubs receive nourishment in the form of chewed up bits of caterpillars by their mother. The fact that they feed on caterpillars makes paper wasps beneficial insects which you want someplace close by, but not necessarily on your house. Paper wasps are not normally aggressive until you disturb their nests. The European paper wasp is far more aggressive than our native paper wasp.

European paper wasp,
Polistes dominulus,

European paper wasp,
Polistes dominulus,

Baldfaced Hornet
(Dolichovespula maculata) is
not a 'true' hornet,
it is in fact a yellowjacket

From Spring on, the queen continually lays eggs and the female workers feed larvae and expand the comb or nest. Each nest can house a few to several dozen paper wasps. They do not eat the protein in the food they gather for the larvae but get their energy from flower nectar. Later in the season, some of the larvae develop into males and others will become next year's queens. The new males and females mate with those of other colonies, and the fertilized females find hiding places under tree bark or in logs and wait out the winter until they can begin their new colony in the spring. The male wasps die in winter; likewise the original nest disintegrates and will not be used again.

Yellowjackets (Vespidae; Vespinae - Vespula spp.)

Yellowjackets are often considered serious pests that have to be eliminated from your property. If you have children playing outside or if you are allergic to stings, then they should be removed.

Because they can be dangerous when disturbed, we recommend using a professional who has the proper safety equipment to remove them.

Control tip: The best way to control Yellowjackets & Paper Wasps:

- Take cotton balls and add a few drops of peppermint oil, attaching them around your property with a thumb pin where wasps like to build nests: Under awnings, porch roofs, under decks. This works in early Spring.

- Another good tool in the Spring is to spray the same locations with Anura Organic Insect Control. Mix 4oz to one gallon of water, repeat in 4 weeks.

- Management of an established Yellowjacket nest is difficult and dangerous to attempt. We recommend you call a professional.

Left – Female Yellowjacket
Right – Male Yellowjacket

BED BUGS (HETEROPTERA)

Bed bugs are small, nearly wingless, flattened bugs that are external parasites of humans. There are other closely related species that feed on bats, cliff swallows, woodpeckers, raptors, chickens and other types of birds. Bed bugs do not transmit any diseases, but they are probably the most profitable bug in the pest control industry. If you made a list of the 100 most dangerous bugs on the planet, bed bugs wouldn't make the list. If you made a list of the top ten most profitable bugs, they would be at the top of the list. You can control bed bugs yourself in your home or business and you don't need toxic pesticides to do so.

The first step in controlling bed bugs is to completely inspect the room to determine the extent of the infestation. Pay close attention to the sleeping areas. They can be hiding anywhere, but they will stay as close to the food source as they can. Small crevices in solid structures, such as the joints in the bed's headboard or between the wall and the baseboard are the bed bugs' refuge of choice. Strip the bed so you can inspect the mattress and box spring. Examine the seams and buttons on the mattress as well as any labels. Bed bugs will hide in all of these areas. Stand the mattress on end if you have to and examine the box spring (if there is one). Stand it up and look at the underside, especially along the edges. Also look behind pictures hanging on the wall, between and behind any books or magazines in close proximity to the bed and in any furniture nearby. You may have to turn some of the furniture over and examine the underside.

Carefully check anything that is under the bed including storage boxes. If there is any litter under the bed, it should be removed. Also check for dried cast skins (exuviae) from the molting process and fecal matter.

Before you start the treatment, there are a few preparations you should do. Wash all the bedding in hot water (120 + degrees). This will kill any bed bugs in the bedding. Personal items such as stuffed animals, blankets, etc. should be vacuumed and placed in plastic bags for a couple of weeks. If you have a clock, phone, radio or other appliance near the bed, they should be opened and inspected as bed bugs will hide in those places as well. Thoroughly vacuum the entire room including inside closets and dresser drawers. If the infestation is severe, you will have to use a crack and crevice vacuum tool to suck the bugs out from along the edge of the carpet, from behind switch plates which you will have to remove, from all around the bed frame, inside the box spring and inside any furniture in the room.

If you see any eggs on the mattress along the seams, you can remove these by picking them up with duct tape and discarding them or brushing them off with a stiff brush. After vacuuming the room or rooms, remove the bag from the vacuum and discard it right away.

Next, use a hair dryer to blow hot air in all the cracks and crevices and along the edge of the carpet and on the furniture to get any bed bugs the vacuuming missed. You want to get as many bed bugs as you can before the final treatment.

Now it is time to treat the bed. Use a flashlight and carefully examine the seams, buttons and any folds in the mattress along with the headboard and footboard if they are present. Check the box spring and frame as well. If you missed any bed bugs with the vacuum or hair dryer, they will be visible. Spray any bed bugs you see with Anura Organic Insect Control concentrate, (mix 4 oz per gallon of water,) as well as all cracks and crevices in the bed. Spray the underside of the box spring as well. If you don't see any bed bugs, then spray along the seams and around the folds and all the other areas mentioned. Make sure to use plenty of solution so the sprayed surface is wet. Then put some diatomaceous earth (DE) in a duster and puff it on all the sprayed areas, including under the box spring. The Anura solution will kill any bed bugs in several minutes and the DE will prevent any from hiding in these areas in the near future.

Now you have to treat all the furniture in the room including night stands, chairs, couches, dressers, etc. Make sure you carefully inspect all the wooden furniture and treat them as you treated the mattress, box spring and bed frame. If any of the furniture, such as bunk beds, have metal framing, treat inside the metal tubing with diatomaceous earth.

Finally, you need to make your bed difficult for bed bugs to access. Tape up any tears in the box spring or mattress with duct tape or, better yet, enclose them in a zippered mattress cover usedfor dust mites. Put the legs of the bed in plastic food bowls or metal cans and coat the inside with Vaseline. Don't let the bed touch any walls or let the bed covers touch the floor.

DIY Tips: How you can trap bed bugs.

- *Placing a heating pad on the floor with sticky traps around it*
  If you don't have sticky traps you can use duct tape, sticky side up.

- *Put an Alka-Seltzer tablet on a damp sponge on a small plate on the heating*
  pad. The Alka-Seltzer will attract any bed bugs in the area.
  This teqhnique also works in catching mosquitoes and fleas; just place two Alka-Seltzer
  tablets in a bowl of soapy water. That usually does the trick.

TICKS (ACARINA)

Ticks are not insects. They are arachnids belonging to the group of mites. They are bigger than all other mites and they are very important. There are hundreds of species of ticks in the world and they are capable of spreading more than 65 diseases, many of them serious. Lyme disease, Rocky Mountain spotted fever, Colorado tick fever and Tularemia are a few.

If someone made a list of the top ten most dangerous pests, ticks would be close to the top of the list. For some reason, they receive almost no attention compared to bed bugs which are absolutely harmless. Ticks mostly feed on the blood of warm-blooded animals, but some species feed on reptiles. They can be found in lawns, yards with trees and shrubs and, occasionally, inside homes. They prefer the shaded areas of your yard.

Medical: If you find a tick imbedded in your pet or on another person or on yourself, do not yank it off. Gently pull the tick straight off with a pair of tweezers. You can also put some diatomaceous earth on the tick and it will come off by itself. Make sure you save the tick so you can get it identified. You want to know what diseases, if any, it can cause. Mark the date of your bite on a calendar and if you develop unusual symptoms in about two weeks, contact your medical professional.

DIY Tips: For controlling ticks in your yard.

- Get a large piece of flannel cloth and tie it to a stick.

- Drag it through the entire yard slowly and pay particular attention to shady areas. Any ticks which are in the yard will get snagged.

- When you're done, put the cloth in a burn barrel and burn it or in a trash bag and seal it shut and take it to the dump.

- Then get some Anura Organic Insect Control concentrate, mix 4 oz per gallon of water, spray to the dripping point all over the shady areas, including along the sides of the house. Spray some all along the foundation where there's dirt abutting the house.

- It takes 30 to 40 days for tick eggs to hatch, so you should repeat this entire process in a month and then again one month later.

If ticks are in your house, you need to treat all the areas where they can hide. This would be behind baseboards, moldings, in furniture and carpets as well as around window sills.

- You can treat these areas with food-grade diatomaceous earth, baking soda, talcum powder. All of these methods will be safe for you and your family and pets but will kill the ticks.

Most of the ticks listed on the next page are only found in the woods and remote areas and won't infest your homes. We are listing them because they can be serious vectors of disease if you should encounter them.

Talaje soft ticks (Ornithodoros talaje)

It feeds on humans, rodents, pigs, cattle, horses. Very painful bite. Found in Arizona, California, Nevada & NM

Medical: It can transmit tick borne relapsing fever in some areas

Herm's soft ticks (Ornithodoros hermsi)

This tick is found in Washington, Oregon, Idaho, California, Nevada, Colorado, Utah and Arizona

Medical: Primary vector of tickborne relapsing fever spirochetes in the area.

Relapsing fever ticks (Argasidae - Ornithodoros turicata)

It feeds on kangaroo rats, rabbits, sheep, cattle, horses, pigs, humans, rattlesnakes and turtles. It is found in New Mexico, Arizona, Colorado, Utah and California.

Medical: May produce intense irritation and swelling at bite site in humans. Also produces relapsing fever spirochetes.

Pajaorella ticks (Argasidae - Ornithodoros coriaceus)

This tick has a very painful bite. There are many tales about the seriousness of the bite and it is feared like a rattlesnake in parts of Mexico. It feeds on humans, deer and swallows.

Lone star ticks (Ixodidae - Amblyomma americanum)

The female Lone star tick has a star-shaped marking on its back, hence its name. They're found from Texas, through the south-central midwest states to the east coast.

Medical: Rocky Mountain spotted fever, ehrlichiosis, tularemia and STARI (Southern Tick Associated Rash Illness).

Gulf coast ticks (Ixodidae - Amblyomma maculatum)

The larvae feed on birds and rodents, while the adults feed on deer & other large mammal. It's found along the Atlantic coast to the Gulf of Mexico.

Medical: It can transmit a form of Rocky Mountain spotted fever as well as canine hepatozoonosis

Rocky Mountain wood ticks (Ixodidae - Dermacentor andersoni)

Rocky Mountain wood tick immatures feed on rodents and rabbits. Adults feed on cattle, sheep, deer, humans and other large mammals. They are found from the western counties of Nebraska and the Black Hills of South Dakota to the Cascade and Sierra Nevada Mountains, and from northern Arizona and northern New Mexico in the United States to British Columbia, Alberta, and Saskatchewan in Canada.

Medical: Rocky mountain spotted fever, tick paralysis and tularemia.

Pacific coast ticks (Ixodidae - Dermacentor occidentalis) Immatures feed on small mammals, adults feed on larger domestic animals, deer and humans. This tick is found in Oregon and California.

Medical: Rocky Mountain spotted fever, tularemia, bovine anaplasmosis, Colorado tick fever, 364D Rickettsiosis.

American dog ticks (Ixodidae - Dermacentor variabilis)

American dog tick immatures feed on small mammals, preferably rodents. Adults feed on domestic dogs and will readily bite humans. They are found throughout the eastern portion of the country as well as in Idaho, Oregon, Washington and California.

Medical: Rocky Mountain spotted fever pathogen and bacterium causing tularemia. It may cause canine paralysis and bovine anaplasmosis and tick paralysis.

Black-legged ticks (Ixodidae - Ixodes spp.)

The female black-legged tick is red and brown, while the male is much darker. They are also known as deer ticks and bear ticks. Immatures feed on various small mammals, birds and lizards. Adults feed on the large mammals such as deer, elk and bears. They will bite humans. **The western black-legged tick (Ixodes pacificus)** is found in Washington, Oregon, California, Idaho, Nevada and Utah. **The eastern black-legged tick (Ixodes scapularis)** is found throughout the eastern United States.

Medical: Both black-legged ticks can transmit Lyme disease as well as anasplasmosis and babesiosis

Brown dog ticks (Ixodidae - Rhipicephalus sanguineus)

Brown dog ticks are found worldwide, mostly in warmer areas. It is small and reddish-brown in color. Females can lay up to 5000 eggs, depending on the amount of blood consumed. Immatures feed on a variety of animals. Adults feed on domestic dogs and occasionally bite humans.

Medical: In dogs, it can transmit canine erhlichiosis and canine babesia. It has recently been identified as a reservoir for Rocky Mountain spotted fever in the southwest.

HEAD AND BODY LICE (PEDICULIDAE - PEDICULUS HUMANUS)

The three main types of lice that infest humans are **the head louse, the body louse** and **the crab louse.** Head lice normally infest the heads of children. Children share these bugs when playing with each other. Body lice will live and breed in clothing and normally infest people who rarely change or wash their clothes. Homeless people frequently get body lice. **Crab lice (Pthiridae – Pthirus pubis)** can infest anyone as they are normally spread by sexual intercourse.

DIY Tips: Simple remedies that work to kill Head and Body Lice:

- *Use a natural coconut oil or olive oil shampoo.*

- *Salt water will also kill lice, so a swim in the ocean would help.*

- *You can put a shower cap on the head and use a hair dryer. The heat from the hair dryer will kill the lice.*

- *Body lice can be controlled by washing the person's clothing and vacuuming any beds or other furniture they may have used. Pesticides aren't necessary.*

- *Crab lice can be controlled with coconut oil or olive oil rubbed into the area where they live. They not only live in the pubic region but can get in armpit hairs and the perianal region as well. Ouch!*

Head and body lice cannot live off the host for more than 48 hours. Crab lice are more dependent on us, as they will die in 24 hours if not on their host. Head and body lice will only attack humans.

FLEAS (SIPHONAPTERA)

Cat and Dog fleas (Pulicidae - Ctenocephalides spp.)

There are many species of fleas throughout North America, but the ones considered pests most often are **dog fleas (Ctenocephalides canis)** and **cat fleas (Ctenocephalides felis),** as these species will infest homes. Other species carry plague and other diseases, but they will not infest a home in large numbers. Dog and cat fleas prefer parts of the country that are humid. They are not established in the arid southwest, although they can turn up when brought in from somewhere else.

DIY Tips: If you have fleas infesting your home, here's what to do:

- *Steam clean the carpets. This will remove dried blood, carpet fibers and other debris, diluted excrement, some flea larvae, eggs, pupal cocoons, adults, feces and other food sources.*

- *You can also use borax or baking soda to kill any fleas, then vacuum.*

- *Spray pets with Anura Botanical Mosquito & Tick Repellent. Available at www.organicpeststore.com.*

To monitor infestations, slowly walk through suspected areas wearing white knee socks. When the fleas jump on you, you should clearly be able to see them on the socks. Or you can put some white pieces of fabric on the floor and the fleas will jump on them.

DIY Tips:

- *Put a goose-neck lamp 8"- 10" over a pan of "fizzy" seltzer water with a few drops of dish soap at night. The fleas are attracted to the heat and carbon dioxide and drown.*

- *Sprinkle salt where animals lie; salt dehydrates the fleas and they die.*

- *You can also dust the carpet with food-grade diatomaceous earth.*

- *Also dust bedding, furniture and other areas your pet frequents. Let the DE set for four days and then vacuum it up.*

- *Also rub some DE through your pet's fur to the skin, especially on the scalp and tail, behind the neck and in any area where your pet can't bite or scratch.*

Caution: *Diatomaceous earth can dry out your pet's skin, so lightly use it no more than once a month.*

- *Borax powder used for boosting cleaning power in laundry can also be used to effectively rid your home of fleas. Borax powder is non-toxic and kills fleas by cutting into their exoskeletons.*

- *The powder can be sprinkled onto carpets and floors where flea infestations exist.*

- *Apply Borax powder to pet bedding and upholstered furniture where pets sleep, in addition to the flooring. Work the borax powder into the surface with a stiff-bristled broom, then vacuum it up.*

Please Note: *Even though borax powder is non-toxic, use caution when young children and pets are around as it can make them sick.*

DIY Tips for outdoors:

- *Outside you can apply nematodes to your yard. You can get nematodes at garden shops where fleas are prevalent. They will reduce the flea population outside by up to 90%. By reducing the outdoor flea population, the likelihood of bringing fleas indoors is reduced.*

FLIES (DIPTERA)

Flies are the fourth largest order of insects and there are over 100,000 species. Most of them are beneficial to some degree as they serve as a food source to many animals and even a few plants. Many breed in organic material such as animal manure and help recycle its nutrients to the soil. Others contribute to the decomposition of dead animals. Flies can also be serious pests. Mosquitoes and other biting flies can cause human deaths by spreading such diseases as malaria, dengue fever, encephalitis, yellow fever and many others. Flies are different from other insects in that they only have a single pair of wings.

If you have a fly problem, a good electric flytrap works well but they are expensive.

DIY Tip: How to make the apple cider vinegar fly trap:

1. Cut the top off several plastic water bottles.

2. Invert the top into the lower portion forming a funnel.

3. Put about two inches of apple cider vinegar in the bottle with a quarter teaspoon of sugar.

Almost all flies, no matter what their normal food preference, will enter the trap.

House flies (Muscidae - Musca domestica)

House flies have a gray thorax (part where head is connected and wings are attached) with four dark stripes, and a mottled abdomen (posterior portion). These flies are considered "filth flies" and will feed on excrement, garbage, carcasses, and even human secretions from wounds and mucous membranes. If you accidentally eat the larvae (maggots) in contaminated food, they can survive in your intestine. They can harbor over 100 different pathogenic organisms and are capable of transmitting more than 65 diseases and bacteria that can cause duodenal and stomach ulcers.

House flies are the most common fly in the World.

When you swat a fly remember to aim your flyswatter about 1½" behind the fly, because when houseflies take of from a horizontal surface, they jump upward and backward.

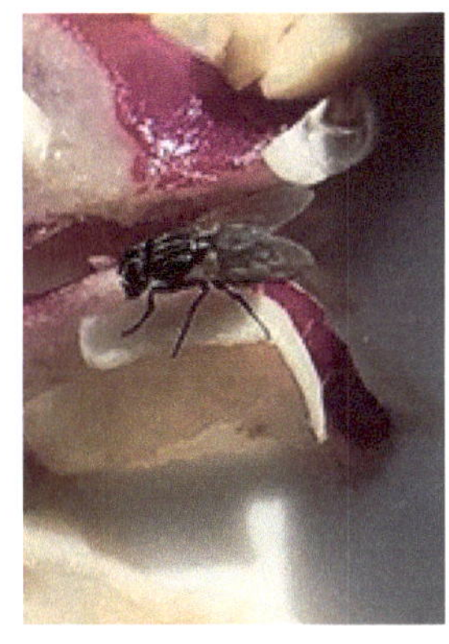

DIY Tips:

• You can set out a saucer filled with bubble soap and apple cider vinegar to attract and kill flies.

• Mix some light Karo Syrup or honey or sugar water with 5% boric acid or borax baits.

Strange, but true: If you fill Ziploc bags with water and hang them around your doors and windows. The sun's refractive light disorients the flies when the sun's rays are shining through the bags. Preventing flies from entering the building. So far, people say these bags work very well.

Little house flies (Fannidae - Fannia canicularia)

Little house flies are dull gray with yellow on the upper abdomen and 3 dark longitudinal stripes on the top of the thorax.

These flies resemble house flies but they fly in circles in the middle of a room or on a porch and don't appear to land. They can lay their eggs in any organic material including compost piles, pet feces, dead leaves, etc. They have been known to enter the urinary tract of naked sleeping persons and cause urinary myiasis. To prevent these flies from appearing, empty and clean all food handling equipment, dishes and garbage containers and daily remove and/or bury all animal droppings, fruit and organic debris inside and/or outside.

DIY Tip: Put two packets of aspartame in 2" of beer in an open container to act as a bait for these flies.

- You can also use a fly swatter with a sticky side to swat them when they are circling.

Cluster flies (Calliphoridae - Pollenia rudis)

Cluster flies are about ½" up to ¾" in size. Slightly larger than the common house flies, they move indoors in the winter in hundreds or even thousands of individuals, hence the name. Unlike house flies, cluster flies are not associated with poor hygiene and poor sanitary conditions. These flies do not carry diseases and other hazards that may affect humans because they do not lay their eggs in human food. They parasitize earthworms in the ground outside. When they invade homes for the winter, they will infest attics, basements, unused rooms, wall voids, ceiling voids and garages.

Control tip: The best way to deal with cluster flies is to prevent them from coming in.

- Check all the obvious entry points.
- Check your windows and doors for small openings.
- Cluster flies can squeeze through the sides of doors and windows, so make sure there isn't enough space for them to pass through.
- Seal or patch cracks and crevices. If you use a screen, make sure there aren't any holes that the insect can go through.

Check your cellar door for possible openings too. These are possible entry points because your basement is an ideal undisturbed spot that cluster flies choose to hibernate in. If you have an attic, do the same. Basically, any room or area in your home that is not visited much by any of the people in your home are the ones you should check.

Blow flies (Calliphoridae-Phormia, Phaenicia, Cynomya & Calliphora)

Blow flies are larger than house flies and are normally shiny green, blue, bronze or black in color. Blow flies feed on decaying animal matter and if you have them in your house it is an indication of a dead animal in the wall or ceiling. Occasionally the only sign of these flies in an early infestation is when the larvae fall from the ceiling void onto the floor. If you can find and remove the carcass of the dead animal they are feeding on, it will speed up the process of them leaving. If you can't, there isn't much you can do except be patient and wait for the dead animal to dry up. They can also lay their eggs in dog feces or any animal matter with a high protein content, including dry cat food. Common names for the most frequently encountered blow flies are **black blow flies, greenbottle flies** and **bluebottle flies.** Greenbottle and bluebottle flies are metallic green or blue in color. Black blow flies have a black sheen.

Fruit flies (Drosophilidae)

Fruit flies are usually found in the kitchen where they feed and breed on food spilled in out-of-the-way places, such as behind or under appliances or similar areas. These small flies have distinctive red eyes, which you can see with a hand lens. They are tan or brown in color and about 1/8" long. They are also known as **pomace flies** and **vinegar flies.** They can be serious pests when found in food handling establishments as they breed in, and feed on fruits, vegetables and any decaying organic material.

Medical: They have been known to cause intestinal problems and diarrhea when fruit containing their larvae is eaten.

They will also breed in discarded fruit juice and soft drink cans and in unsecured bottles of wine. They are also very prolific as the female can lay about 500 eggs which will hatch in as little as eight days.

These little flies are also beneficial as they have been studied in research in genetics. This research became the foundation on which future genetic research was built.

Control tip: *In your home you can control fruit flies by totally eliminating all breeding material.*

- *They are attracted to acetic acid (vinegar), so put some drops on duct tape or glue boards.*
- *Or you can fill a small paper cup with vinegar and the flies will just dive in.*

Hump-backed flies (Phoridae)

Phorids are small flies, about 1/8" long and tan to dark brown in color. They have a distinct hump-backed shape thorax, hence their common name. They do not have red eyes as fruit flies do. When these flies are disturbed, they will run along the surface they are on rather than flying away.

These flies breed in any moist organic material including dirty mops, garbage, decaying fruits and vegetables and dead animal matter. They are also known as coffin flies because of their presence where dead bodies are found, including inside of coffins. There are over 220 species of phorid flies in the United States.

Control tip: *You have to eliminate the food source and breeding areas in order to control them in your home or business.*

Dung flies (Sphaeroceridae)

Sphaerocerid flies are sometimes called dung flies, but that name probably isn't appropriate. While they will breed in dung, they will also breed in other organic materials and are often found in areas where **phorid** or **drosophilid flies** breed. Sphaerocerids can be recognized by the enlarged size of the first tarsal segment on their hind legs. The tarsi are the last five segments on the leg. They are very small, about an 1/8 of an inch and dark-colored. There are over 240 species of sphaerocerids in the United States and they are easily transported around the country as they will frequently breed in decaying material carried in commerce.

These flies will breed in organic material spilled in cracks in the floor, unclean trash containers and even the bottom of elevator shafts if it is damp and has decaying organic matter there. They can be a problem in food establishments if there is a lot of spilled food that works its way into floor cracks or expansion joints.

Control tip: *The best way to control these flies is to find out where they are breeding and totally eliminate the decaying material from the area.*

Moth flies (Psychodidae)

These small flies sometimes called filter flies or drain flies have hairy wings that resemble small moths. They breed in the gunk buildup in bathroom drains and will often be found in the tub, on shower curtains or the wall just hopping around. The larvae live in gelatinous material in sink and floor drain traps, in sewer treatment plants and in septic tanks. You can also find them in damp crawl spaces under a house.

Control tip:
- *Keep drains clean to control these flies as they have a very short life cycle.*
- *To determine which drain the moth flies are breeding in you can put duct tape sticky side down over the suspect drain.*

Note: They can go from egg to adult in a little over a week in some areas.

Fungus Gnats (Sciaridae)

Fungus gnats are very small flies with long legs and long antennae and distinctly patterned wings. They are dark brown or black in color. They are generally found in over-watered house plants where the larvae feed on fungus in the potting soil and moist organic material.

Control tip: *The best way to control them is to let the plants dry out almost to the point of wilting before re-watering.*
This will kill the larvae in the soil.

- *For potted-plants, put an inch of aquarium gravel on the soil to prevent female fungus gnats from laying any more eggs in the potting soil.*
- *You can also place a yellow sticky trap on a stick in the soil to catch the adult gnats.*

Mosquitoes (Culicidae)

Mosquitoes are the most deadliest biting creatures on earth. Their bite sucks out our blood and spits out a chemical that prevents the blood from clotting, often leaving a parting gift of a virus or parasite. Trash can provide enough water to lay their eggs. They can transmit West Nile Virus, Encephalitis, and many other diseases. If you have mosquitoes, make sure you wear a good non-DEET mosquito repellent. DEET works well as long as it is full strength. However, when it begins to weaken, it can actually attract mosquitoes and you have to put more on, which means absorbing more of the chemicals into your system. Most non-DEET products (Cedar- wood oil, catnip, citronella, and lemongrass) are effective for two or three hours before having to be reapplied, but they do not contain potentially harmful chemicals, nor do they attract the insects.

Outdoor control tips:

- *Remove all standing or stagnant water if at all possible.*

- *Remove old tires, barrels, cans, wading pools that aren't being used, bird baths and other items that can hold water.*

- *Apply a light coating of food-grade diatomaceous earth on any water that can't be removed.*

- *Eucalyptus oils, garlic extracts and extracts of orange and lemon peels will kill mosquito larvae in the water.*

If you have adult mosquitoes in your grass or bushes, you can spray them with Anura Organic Insect Control, (mix 4 oz per gallon of water.)

- *Catnip is a good repellent according to a report from Iowa State University.*

- *Other good repellents include lemongrass, basil, birch, mint, rosemary, spearmint and yarrow.*

- *Geraniums or basil plants planted near your doors will repel mosquitoes.*

- *Please note: Citronella and pennyroyal both work but have side affects. Pennyroyal may increase the risk of a miscarriage if you are pregnant and citronella has been known to attract female black bears. Test anything you put on your skin on a small portion first to make sure you aren't allergic to it.*

Control tip for protecting yourself & kids:

The best way to repel mosquitoes is to cover yourself with Anura Botanical Mosquito & Tick Repellent. It's only available online at: organicpeststore.com

MOTHS (LEPIDOPTERA)

There are several types of moths that can become household pests. Clothes moths can damage clothing and pantry moths can infest some stored foods. Other moths that come in the house are occasional invaders and won't do any damage.

Clothes moths (Tineidae)

There are two distinct types of clothes moths commonly found in homes. They are both small moths. **The webbing clothes moth (Tineola bisselliella)** is a solid golden brown on the wings, while **the casemaking clothes moth (Tinea pellionella)** has three black spots on each wing. Casemaking clothes moth larvae construct a small bag from fabric to protect their body from the environment. They drag the bag or tube wherever they feed.

Clothes moths are occasionally found in closets where they lay their eggs on suitable fabric. The larvae hatch and feed on the fabric doing damage.

Control tip: Several things you can do to prevent clothes moths.

- First, keep clothes and other fabrics stored in sealed, plastic bags.

- Next, you can hang some repellents in the closets. Put dried lemon peels, cedar chips, dried rosemary or mint in cheese cloth bags and hang them in the closets.

- Make sure any carpets in the closet are clean and free of lint or animal hair or any organic debris.

- If you already have webbing clothes moths, you should hang one Clothes Moth Pheromone Trap in each closet. This will attract and catch the male moths and stop the breeding process.

Note: Don't hang more than one trap or you will confuse the moths and they will just fly around, not sure where to go. The pheromone traps aren't effective against casemaking clothes moths.

- Dry cleaning or washing all infested clothing in hot, soapy water will kill all the stages of the moths including the larvae & eggs.

Indian meal moths (Pyralidae - Plodia interpunctella)

There are several species of pantry moths that can infest your home, but the one most frequently encountered is the Indian meal moth. This moth is small and colorful. The wings are gray toward the body and has dark bands near the tip.

They will feed on a wide variety of dried foods, including cereals, flour, cornmeal, crackers, cake mixes, pasta, dried pet foods, candy, powdered milk, chocolate candy and many other foodstuffs.

Control tip: The best control is to hang one Flour Moth Pheromone Trap in the area they are infesting. This will attract and catch the male moths and stop the breeding process.

1. Inspect all open dried foods and toss anything that is infested.
2. Place all non-infested foods in sealed containers or refrigerate them.
3. Completely clean the pantry where the foods are stored to get any larvae that may be crawling around.

STINKBUGS (PENTATOMIDAE)

Boxelder bugs (Boisea trivittata)

Generally not considered a pest, they can become a nuisance however, clustering in large numbers and entering parts of the home in search of food and water in the autumn. They belong to the Stinkbug family.

Boxelder bugs feed almost entirely on seeds of boxelder, maple and ash trees. They are easy to identify with nymphs having bright red coloration, the adults are dark brown about half inch long with red markings on their wing tips.

Control tips: The best method for controlling Boxelder bugs:

* Spray them outside before they have the chance to move inside the home.
* Use Anura Organic Insect Control. Mix 4 oz to one gallon of water and spray insects directly as a contact killer.
* Spray exterior of the home that receives most sun, from the foundation at least 4 feet up, and repeat in 2 weeks to give your home a lasting repellency.
* Dust around windowsills with diatomaceous earth.

BEETLES (COLEOPTERA)

There are three groups of beetles that can cause problems in a home. Carpet beetles will damage carpets, clothing, animal fur, feathers & similar products. Stored product beetles will infest many dried foods and wood boring beetles can damage the structure of a home or wooden objects in it.

Carpet Beetles (Dermestidae)

Carpet beetle larvae are small, about 1/4" long and carrot-shaped with long hairs. They will feed on anything organic. The adult beetles are small, round and usually black in color, sometimes with lighter markings.

> **Control tips:** The best method for controlling carpet beetles is by completely cleaning everything:
> - *Steam clean the carpets as well as any upholstered furniture.*
> - *Make sure you vacuum under all furniture. Carpet beetles can survive by feeding on dust bunnies.*
> - *If you don't mind the smell of Cedar oil—Keep a bottle Anura Organic Insect Control. (mix 4 oz per gallon of water.) available to directly spray any adults or larvae you find.*
> - *Make sure you vacuum up all the dead insects as the spines on the carpet beetle larvae can penetrate your pores, causing rashes.*

Also, adult carpet beetles feed on the nectar in flowers so they don't do any damage beyond breeding indoors. If you have flowers blooming near your house, you will attract adult carpet beetles. Make sure there aren't any ways for them to get into your house.

Flour beetles (Tenebrionidae – Tribolium spp.)

Flour beetles are small, brownish in color and elongated. There are nine species that are potential pests in stored food products. Two species are very common. **The confused flour beetle (Tribolium confusum)** is common in northern regions and **the red flour beetle (Tribolium castaneum)** is more common in southern areas. They feed on barley, beet pulp, breakfast cereals, grains, nuts, wheat, wheat bran, milk chocolate, dried milk and occasionally hides.

> **Control tips:** Good sanitation is key to controlling these beetles.
> - *Freezing stored products at -4 degrees for 24 hours will kill all stages.*
> - *Heating at 122 degrees for an hour is also very effective.*

Drugstore beetles (Anobiidae – Stegobium paniceum)

These beetles have a hood-like thorax which hides the head when viewed from above. They are reddish brown in color and rounded in profile and oval-shaped. They feed on a variety of products including tobacco, seeds, grain, nuts, beans, spices, dried fruits and vegetables, flour, rice, ginger, yeast, herbs, paprika, dry dog and cat food, cocoa, biscuits, raisins, dates, alfalfa, hay, almond hulls, barley, corn meal, rice meal, wheat bran and even rodenticides. They are good at penetrating food packaging.

Control tip: Use same control methods for flour beetles on this species.

Saw-toothed grain beetles (Silvanidae – Oryzaephilus surinamensis)

Saw-toothed grain beetles are small, black, elongated and have six distinct saw-like teeth on each side of the thorax. They are commonly associated with breakfast cereals and are frequently found in corn meal, flour, biscuit mix and processed cereals as well as in alfalfa seed, almonds, baking soda, barley, candy, clover seeds, chocolate, sugar, rice, wheat, cereals, dried fruits, corn, cornmeal, corn starch, flour, garbanzos, hay, honeycomb, milo, mixed feeds, oats, raisins, rice, figs, peas, pecans, dried meat and tobacco. Sanitation and freezing and heating will also work on these beetles.

Hide & Larder beetles (Dermestidae – Dermestes spp.)

Dermestid beetles are larger than other stored product beetles, reaching 1/3" long. The hide beetle is brown on top and white on the bottom. The larder beetle is brown with a broad cream-colored band across the front of the abdomen. These beetles prefer animal products such as leather goods, hides, skins, dried fish, pet food, bacon, cheese and feathers. They can be a major pest in museums.

Control tip: Sanitation is important
- Sticky traps can be used on flat surfaces to catch adult and larval dermestid beeetles.

Weevils (Curculionidae – Sitophilus spp.)

Weevils are easily recognized by their small size and prominent snout. They are very destructive to stored grains. They will feed on chick peas, corn, oats, barley, rye, wheat, kafir, buckwheat and millet. They are frequently found in macaroni and noodles. When you find any of these beetles in your home, inspect all open dried foods and toss anything that is infested. Place all non-infested foods insealed containers.

Control tip: Completely clean the pantry where the foods are stored.
- Lightly dust the shelves with food-grade diatomaceous earth.

False powder post beetles (Anobiidae & Bostrichidae)

There are a number of species of beetles in this family that attack wood. They will attack new and old hardwoods and softwoods, with as little as a 12% moisture content. They are recognized by their hood-like thorax that hides the head when viewed from above. They have a cylindrical body shape and are reddish-brown to brownish-black in color. They are often found infesting wood joists and sill plates in crawl spaces under homes. Two common species are **the deathwatch beetle (Xestobium rufovillosum)** and **the furniture beetle (Anobium punctatum).** The furniture beetle will infest furniture and pine flooring.

Other beetles in these two families include **the California deathwatch beetle (Hadrobregmus gibbicollis)** which occurs along the Pacific Coast. **Xyletinus pelatus** is found in the eastern United States and attacks cellar joists and flooring in damp buildings. **Nicobium castaenum** is found in Virginia, South Carolina to Louisiana and attacks furniture and pine woodwork. **The lead cable borer (Scobicia declivis)** normally infests dead and seasoning oak and damage can be severe. It is found throughout the west and is most common in California.

> **Control tip:** The best method of control for all wood-boring beetles:
> - *Treat all exposed wood with sodium borate, which will prevent them from reinfesting the wood after they emerge.*

Powder post beetles (Bostrichinae; Lyctinae – Lyctus spp.)

Powder post beetles are small, elongated and almost always infest hardwoods. They frequently infest lumber, woodwork, furniture, tool handles, gun stocks and similar items. They produce very fine, powder-like frass when they damage wood. Frass from anobiids and bostrichids is not nearly as fine as these beetles produce. They are second only to termites in destructive capability. There are several destructive species nationwide.

The brown powder-post beetle (Lyctus brunneus) can be found in most states and is frequently found infesting imported hardwood products.

The western powder-post beetle (Lyctus cavicollis) is found throughout the United States and attacks oak firewood and hickory, orange and eucayptus wood. **The European powder-post beetle (Lyctus linearis)** is found in the eastern United States and attacks hickory, oak, ash, walnut and wild cherry wood.

The southern powder-post beetle (Lyctus planicollis) is found nationwide but does most of its damage in the southern states. It prefers seasoned or partially seasoned wood of oak, ash and hickory.

The white-marked powder-post beetle (Trogoxylon parallelopipedum) is a common native species and has the same food preferences as the southern powder-post beetle.

Long-horned borers (Cerambycidae)

Only a few species of long-horned beetles are pests of wood in homes.
The old house borer (Hylotrupes bajulus) is probably the most destructive species in this family of beetles. It is found from Maine to Florida and west to Michigan, and south to Texas. There have been some reports of this beetle in California. They are between ½" and ¾" long and are slightly flattened. They are brownish-black in color. Each wing cover has a gray band on it.

They are usually built into a house with wood from storage as adults have been found at lumber mills in seasoned and unseasoned wood. The frass is slightly granular and composed of small, barrel-shaped pellets of digested wood and irregular shaped wood fragments that were not eaten. The larvae can feed on the wood from 2 to 10 years before maturing into adulthood, depending on environmental conditions.

Metallic wood borers (Buprestidae)

The larval form of these beetles are called flat-headed borers, because the exit holes in the wood are oval, not round as in most other wood boring beetle larvae. Only a few species will attack seasoned wood, so they aren't a serious
pests. The adult beetles are often brightly colored and metallic. With a boat shaped appearance.

The most destructive species is **the golden metallic borer (Buprestis aurulenta).** The wings are greenish-blue with copper margins. They will attack flooring and woodwork of Douglas Fir that isn't finished with paint or varnish. They also feed on pine and spruce lumber. These beetles are found throughout the western United States.

Control tip: The best method of control for all wood-boring beetles:

- *Treat all exposed wood with sodium borate, which will prevent them from reinfesting the wood after they emerge.*

TERMITES (ISOPTERA)

There are over 50 species of termites in the United States, but only a few species of subterranean termites and drywood termites are serious pests.

Drywood termites (Kalotermidae – Incisitermes spp.)

Drywood termites do not need soil contact. They live in dry, sound wood, usually near the surface. They get what moisture they require from the wood they feed on and from the water formed during digestion of that wood. Drywood swarmers generally enter your home at night through unscreened attic or foundation vents or through cracks and crevices between exposed wood. Drywood termites are most commonly recognized by their distinctive fecal pellets (piles) that are often the color of the wood they are feeding upon. The fecal pellets are kicked out of the wood by the nymphs (workers) through "kick holes" that are visible.

Incisitermes minor is found in much of California where it is a major pest. It is also found in Arizona, Utah and New Mexico.

Incisitermes snyderi, Incisitermes schwarzi and **Kalotermes approximatus** are species found in the southeastern states that are of economic importance because of the damage they are capable of doing.

Control tip: Call in a pest-control professional. This is a serious matter. Make sure they use XT-2000 Orange oil.

Subterranean termites (Rhinotermitidae)

Subterranean termites are social insects with very large colonies. They consist of a queen, sexual reproductives, workers and soldiers. The workers are grayish or white and wingless. They are the ones in the colony that forage for food. They also groom the queens, eggs, nymphs and soldiers and build the nest. Workers are the ones who do the damage to the wood. The workers have a mass of unique protozoa in their lower digestive tract and it is these protozoans that enable the termites to digest wood. When the protozoans are killed, the termites will quickly starve and the entire colony will die off as the workers feed the other caste members in the colony through a process call trophallaxis.

Control tip: Subterranean termites share their food between members of the same colony, making commercial products that contain antibiotics and borates very effective. A pest-control professional is needed for this task.

Western subterranean termites (Reticulitermes hesperus)

The western subterranean termite is found from British Colombia south to western Mexico and is very common along the Pacific coastal areas. It occurs as far east as Idaho and Nevada. Their colonies can reach several hundred thousand individuals and the colony has to be about three years old before they can swarm. They do extensive damage and will attack fence posts, utility poles, any wood and living plants and trees.

Eastern subterranean termites (Reticulitermes flavipes)

The eastern subterranean termite is the most destructive species in this group. It is found throughout the eastern United States and is found as far west as eastern New Mexico. It occurs in spotty areas of Utah and Arizona as well. It has very large colonies numbering ¼ million individuals. They go below the frost line during extreme cold weather. They build earth-like shelter tubes over obstacles like the desert subterranean termite.

Arid land subterranean termites (Reticulitermes tibialis)

This is the arid land subterranean termite. It is found in arid desert areas and higher elevations and ranges from Oregon and Montana, south to Mexico and eastward to Missouri, Arkansas and Texas. This is the most common termite in New Mexico. It is the least destructive of the termites in this group, although it can cause considerable damage in some situations.

Desert subterranean termites (Heterotermes aureus)

This is the desert subterranean termite. It is found in desert regions of southern Arizona and California. It is common in the Phoenix area but not as common near Tucson. This termite is very destructive. It will attack sound dry wood, utility poles and posts. It will build earth-like tube shelters over obstacles to get to edible wood.
The western subterranean and arid land termites do not build these tube-like shelters.

Formosan subterranean termites (Coptotermes formosanus) Formosan

termites are larger than our native subterranean termites. Originally introduced from Asia on ships. They are very destructive, attacking all kinds of wood and cellulose products. Living plants will also be attacked when moisture is not available anywhere else.

They have been known to hollow a building wall in three months.
Evidence of their presence are channels between pieces of wood. Channels or dirt-colored tubes are usually built on foundations. They do not have to maintain ground contact, so a normal subterranean treatment may not be effective.
Formosan termites are established in Hawaii and have been introduced in Texas, Louisiana and South Carolina and isolated areas in California.

Scorpions and centipedes are two groups of arthropods that nobody wants in their homes. Both of these animals have the capability of stinging you or biting you with painful results. Only one species of scorpion in this country is dangerously venomous. It is **the bark scorpion (Centruroides sculpturatus)** found mostly in Arizona but also southwestern New Mexico. It has killed a few people in Arizona, but not in the last 40 years. Centipede bites are painful, but not deadly in this country. However, anyone can be allergic.

There are over two hundred species of centipedes in the western U.S., but most of them are very small and belong to two suborders. They are **the stone centipedes (Lithobiomorpha)** and **the soil centipedes (Geophilomorpha).** Stone centipedes are about an inch long and have 15 pair of legs. Soil centipedes aren't much longer and have upwards of 40 pair of legs. Neither group is capable of biting people. Both are common in yards and feed on small bugs including some pests, so they can be considered beneficial. **House centipedes (Scutigera coleoptrata)** are about an inch long and have 15 pair of very long legs. They are common almost everywhere and are often found in homes. They rarely bite and they do feed on such pests as spiders, bed bugs, termites, cockroaches, ants and silverfish, so they should probably be welcome in the home.

Three species of **Scolopendromorpha centipedes** are found in the western states. **The desert centipede (Scolopendra polymorpha)** is most common throughout the west with the exception of Washington. It is about three or four inches long. **The green centipede (Scolopendra viridis)** is found in the mountainous areas of New Mexico, Arizona, southeastern Colorado, Utah and extreme southern Nevada. It is only a couple of inches long. **The giant desert centipede (Scolopendra heros)** is found in the southern and eastern portions of New Mexico, much of Arizona and the extreme southeast portion of Colorado. This species can reach a length of 6.5 inches and is capable of killing and eating mice. All of the Scolopendra have painful bites but they are not dangerous.

Centipedes and scorpions are usually found in areas of high moisture such as loose bark, in rotting logs, under stones, boards, railroad ties, trash, piles of leaves and grass clippings and similar areas. They are nocturnal or active at night and hide by day in the earth, wandering forth by night to hunt. They occasionally invade structures and will feed on cockroaches, crickets, spiders, etc. Although they may be found anywhere in a building, including beds, the usual places are damp basements, bathrooms, and any crawl space under the home or building.

Outside the home, firewood should be stacked on racks off the soil and kept outside until immediately ready to burn. Garbage cans should be on racks to elevate them. Grass should be mowed to prevent hiding areas for scorpions.

Exterior control tip: Exclusion to keep them out is the key.

- First step is to examine the entire exterior.
- Cut any tree or shrub branches that touch the structure.
- Fill in any cracks or openings found with caulk and ensure all vent screens are in place and in good condition.
- Spray surounding foundation with (4 fl oz per gallon of water,) Anura Organic Insect Control concentrate.
- In the yard you can eliminate many potential harborage sites for scorpions & centipedes such as rocks, boards, and other objects resting on the soil.
- Dust any loose bark on trees with food grade diatomaceous earth.

Interior control tip: If you find a scorpion or centipede in your home.

- Spray it with Anura Organic Insect Control.
- Don't use synthetic pesticides as they can be more harmful to inhabitants than the scorpion or centipede.

SPIDERS (ARACHNIDA)

Most spiders possess venom glands, however very few spiders can break the skin with their fangs. All spiders will bite in self-defense, such as being squeezed. Most bites occur when people roll over in bed, or when they put on their clothes and a spider inside the clothing bites. Not all spiders are harmless. Black widows and brown recluse are certainly capable of producing a serious bite and any such bite by these spiders should be considered a major medical emergency. Sac spiders and wolf spiders can give serious, though not fatal bites, particularly if you are allergic to the venom. **Daddy longlegs (or harvestmen)** are not at all dangerous despite their reputation to the contrary. Jumping spiders are harmless. Most of the small hunting spiders, such as ground spiders, are incapable of hurting anyone.

Control tip:

- *Around your home you can dust the bottom of the baseboard with food-grade diatomaceous earth to create an effective spider barrier.*

- *If you have a stray spider you need to kill, use a natural product like Anura Organic Insect Control. This product will kill young in the egg sack.*

Black widow spiders (Theridiidae – Latrodectus spp.)

There are three main species in the black widow group. **The eastern black widow (Latrodectus mactans), the western black widow (Latrodectus hesperus) and the brown widow (Latrodectus geometricus)** The eastern black widow is found throughout the east with the exception of Maine, New Hampshire and most of Vermont. The western black widow is found in every state west of central North Dakota south to Texas. The brown widow is found in Florida and Texas. All the female widow spiders have a reddish hourglass-shaped marking on the underside of a shiny black abdomen. The abdomen is brown in the brown widow.

Medical: The black widow is feared everywhere but isn't as dangerous as we're told. The toxic venom is neurotoxic, but the spider injects very little material and the death rate is about 1%. Additionally, the black widow is not inclined to bite unless it is squeezed or defending its egg sac in a web. I pick them up all the time and have never had one try to bite me.

False black widows (Theridiidae – Steatoda grossa)

The false black widow is often mistaken for the real black widow. They are about the same size and the same color. The false black widow does not have the red hourglass marking on its abdomen. It usually has a yellowish band across the front portion of its abdomen on top. It originally came from Europe and is found along both coasts, the states that border the Great Lakes and has been found in Colorado, Arizona and New Mexico as well as a few other inland states. It is absolutely harmless and like the real black widow, it is non-aggressive.

Recluse spiders (Sicariidae – Loxosceles spp.)

The brown recluse spider (Loxosceles reclusa) is shy, sedentary and builds an irregular web that is often not even recognized as a spiderweb. It has a fiddle-shaped pattern on its cephalothorax. Females lay eggs in flattened egg sacs that are frequently attached to the underside of objects. When they are indoors, they can usually be found in dark places, beneath or behind furniture, in boxes or storage areas, among stored books and papers and similar areas. Outside they live under rocks, boards and other dark areas.

The brown recluse is found from eastern areas of the country west to Texas, Oklahoma and eastern New Mexico. It is frequently transported to different parts of the country by commercial vehicles or luggage. There are several other species of Loxosceles in the southwest. None of them have bitten anyone so it's unknown if they're harmful or not. One species introduced into California and Massachusetts, Loxosceles laeta, is potentially dangerous.

Medical: Brown Recluse bites are not painful at the time of the bite. After an hour or so there may be intense pain where bitten. There is usually a dark depressed area at the site of the bite which will turn darker in a day or so. The dead tissue will slough away and the bite area will scar over. Death seldom, if ever occurs, but the bite is extremely debilitating and traumatic. If you know you were bitten by a brown recluse, seek medical attention right away.

Control tip: A few suggestions to control spiders around your home:

- *Control the lighting at night that attracts flying insects.*

- *If you have firewood, stack it somewhere where there is a lot of sunlight and cover it with black plastic. It will get so hot under there that spiders will cook.*

- *Seal any cracks or crevices around the house that would let hunting spiders inside. If your doors do not close tightly, install door sweeps.*

- *Make sure your bed isn't touching the wall. This will make it hard for spiders to get into bed with you.*

- *Don't leave clothing on the floor. Completely shake it out before putting it on.*

Hobo spiders (Agelenidae – Tegenaria agrestis)

The Hobo Spiders are in the genus Tegenaria. Tegenaria agrestis was first introduced into the ports of Seattle in the late 1920s and has been moving south ever since. It is now found in Washington, Oregon, Idaho, Western Montana and much of Utah. They originally came from Europe where they are most common in homes. Generally, these spiders are yellow to pale tan in color with long legs. These spiders occur in highest frequency in July through September and reproduce during this period. Females produce an egg sac that is placed near the opening of the funnel in their webs.

Medical: The bite of this species is not considered to be as dangerous as that of either the brown recluse or widow spiders. Its bite can cause redness, and can involve some systemic reactions. In the latest research from the Oregon Health and Science University, venom has so far not been shown to cause necrotic tissue death of the skin, despite claims to the contrary.

Hobo Spider
Tegenaria agrestis

Common house spiders (Agelenidae – Tegenaria domestica)

This may be one of the most common spiders found in homes in the country. It is found in every state, most Canadian provinces and virtually all over the world. The cephalothorax (section where legs are attached) is shiny brown with two longitudinal stripes running down the middle. The abdomen is grayish with a series of chevron shaped markings running down the middle to the end. The legs are brownish-gray with black bands. The similar and more aggressive hobo spider does not have bands on its legs. The common house spider is harmless and feeds on a lot of household pest insects, so it can be considered beneficial.

Orb-weaver spiders (Araneidae)

Orb-weavers (family Araneidae) are large spiders that make distinct orb-like webs that are often very close to homes. Occasionally the webs are attached to a home. **The pumpkin spider,** which is large, has two humps and a distinct pattern, often scares people. It is common in many areas and is absolutely harmless.

Ground spiders (Gnaphosidae)

Ground spiders (family Gnaphosidae) are very common and are frequently found indoors. They live under debris on the ground outside and often accidentally wander into homes. Most of them are completely harmless.

One species, **eastern parson spider (Herpyllus ecclesiasticus),** can give a painful, but not dangerous bite. Some people suffer allergic reactions to the bite. This spider is about ½" long, blackish with a distinctive white or pink pattern on the middle of it's back. The marking resembles an old-style cravat worn by clergy in the 18th century. This spider is found almost everywhere east of the Rocky Mountains. A similar species, **the western parson spider (Herpyllus propinquus)** is found west of the mountains.

Sac spiders (Clubionidae – Cheiracanthium spp.)

Sac spiders are responsible for spider bites in homes more often than most other species. It's possible many sac spider bites are blamed on the recluse. Two species are referred to as yellow sac spiders due to their similar coloration. They are **Cheiracanthium inclusum** and **C. mildei.** They are light yellowish to a pale yellowish-green, sometimes with an orange- brown stripe on top of the abdomen. They are small, ¼" to 3/8" long. **Yellow sac spiders** are found throughout the country. Female sac spiders build a silken sac in a protected area, often under furniture.

Medical: They usually come out at night to hunt and that is when most bites take place. Usually the bite comes with a sharp pain, resulting in swelling and the possibility of systemic symptoms, some that can last for up to 5 days or more.

Jumping spiders (Salticidae)

Jumping spiders are easily distinguished from other spiders by their four big eyes on the face and four smaller eyes on top of the head. In the U. S. there are at least 40 genera and more than 300 species.

There is one species of jumping spiders **Phidippus audax** that can be mistaken for the Black Widow. These spiders are 1/8" - 3/4" long with robust, relatively short legs. They are mostly black with white or red markings on the dorsal surface of the abdomen. Another species, **Phidippus formosus** has been reported to bite, causing only a mild irritation, e.g., localized swelling and sensitivity. These beneficial spiders hunt and pounce on flies and other insect pests and eat them, liking sunny areas on porches and walls.

Wolf spiders (Lycoside - Lycosa spp)

Wolf spiders are robust and agile hunting spiders with excellent eyesight. They occasionally enter homes and garages and can be found almost anywhere inside. They can be from ½" to 2" in length, depending on the species. They are hairy, grayish or brown, with various markings on the back. The females are often seen carrying around her egg sac and then her babies on her back. Wolf spiders are not dangerous at all but will bite like any spider if it is squeezed or mishandled.

Arizona Blond
Tarantula

Tarantulas (Theraphosidae)

Tarantulas are very large hunting spiders. You often see the males crossing the road after a rain. They are looking for females to mate with. Although they are fearsome looking, they are not at all dangerous. A large one can deliver a painful bite if molested, but they are not lethal.

In the Americas, the term "tarantula" refers to any of about 300 species of primitive spiders with poor eyesight. About 30 species occur in the United States. Many are among the largest of all spiders, weighing 2 - 3 oz. and with a 10" leg spread. The term "tarantula" is derived from a city in Italy and actually belongs to a wolf spider of that area, Lycosa tarentula. Immigrants who saw the big American spiders called them tarantulas. Female tarantulas have been known to live up to 25 years in captivity, while males only live for a year after it reaches maturity.

Josh McCloud is a very successful Organic Pest Control business owner in Missoula Montana. He's been helping people solve their pest problems for over 15 years.
It's his passion for using natural pest control products that compelled him to create the—Concerned Citizens Safe Pest Control Guide. His understanding of how to use natural pest control products has the interest and respect of professionals from around the world. We hope that you find this Pest Guide helpful.

Josh lives with his wife and three kids in Missoula Montana.

Please visit our website for our organic insect pest control and our personal Mosquito and Tick repellent at: organicpeststore.com

Or like us on Facebook @Anurapestproducts

Notes